My Mom Votes!

Louie Simpson

INFOMAX COMMON CORE READERS

Rosen Classroom™

New York

Published in 2013 by The Rosen Publishing Group, Inc.
29 East 21st Street, New York, NY 10010

Book Design: Michael Harmon

Photo Credits: Cover Hill Street Studios/Blend Images/Getty Images; pp. 4, 22 Hemera/Thinkstock.com;
p. 5 Jupiterimages/Thinkstock.com; p. 6 Digital Vision./Thinkstock.com; p. 7 Andy Sacks/Stone/Getty Images;
pp. 8, 17 iStockphoto/Thinkstock.com; p. 9 Giulio Marcocchi/Stringer/Getty Images Entertainment/Getty Images;
p. 10 Digital Vision./Digital Vision/Getty Images; p. 11 Comstock/Comstock Images/Getty Images; p. 12 Stephen Colburn/
Shutterstock.com; p. 13 Karin Hildebrand Lau/Shutterstock.com; p. 14 withGod/Shutterstock.com; p. 16 UpperCut
Images/UpperCut Images/Getty Images; p. 18 Jupiterimages/Workbook Stock/Getty Images; p. 19 Ryan Rodrick Beiler/
Shutterstock.com; p. 20 FPG/Staff/Archive Photos/Getty Images; p. 21 Mike Flippo/Shutterstock.com.

ISBN: 978-1-4488-9055-2
6-pack ISBN: 978-1-4488-9056-9

Manufactured in the United States of America

CPSIA Compliance Information: Batch #WS12RC: For further information contact Rosen Publishing, New York, New York at 1-800-237-9932.

Word Count: 440

Contents

All About Voting 4

Our Leaders 8

Going to Vote 12

Where We Vote 15

Who Can Vote? 18

Glossary 23

Index 24

All About Voting

Do you know what it means to vote? Voting means that you pick something. When you vote for something, you pick it above all other things.

Sometimes, we vote in school. We vote to tell our teacher what we want to do or what games we want to play.

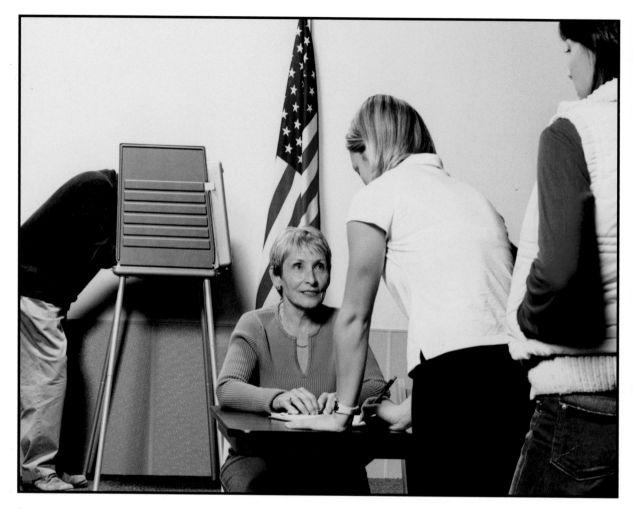

I asked my mom if she votes. She votes to elect the leaders of our country. Electing something means that many people voted for it.

My mom says that voting is important because it lets us decide who leads our country. Our leaders make rules and laws. Rules and laws tell us how to live.

Our Leaders

The most important leader in our country is the president. We elect a president every 4 years. Do you know when the next president will be elected?

We also have leaders in our towns and cities. Each state has leaders, too. We vote to make these people our leaders.

Many people want to be leaders. People who want to be elected are called **candidates**. Candidates spend a lot of time talking to people.

Each candidate has different ideas about how to make our country great. They make **speeches** to tell us about their ideas.

Going to Vote

My mom learns about every candidate. She likes to know how every person feels. This helps her decide who to vote for.

On **Election** Day, my mom wakes up really early. She
votes before work. Some of her friends vote
during the day. My mom votes at a building
in my town.

My mom uses a voting **booth**. The voting booth keeps her vote secret. Nobody else can see whom she picks. This makes our elections fair.

Where We Vote

On Election Day, we vote at many places.

Where do your parents vote?

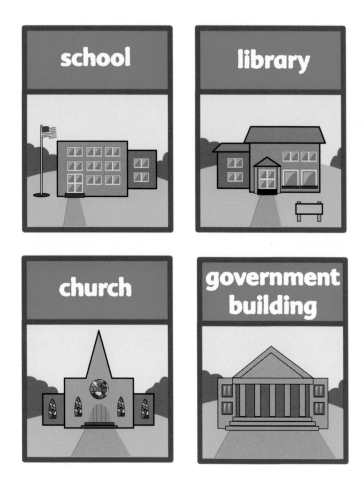

school

library

church

government building

My mom votes for the candidate she agrees with the most. The candidate who gets the most votes wins the election!

My mom is happy that she can vote. Voting can change something we don't like. It can also make good things happen.

Who Can Vote?

If you want to vote, you must be 18 or older. You must also be a citizen. That means you were born in the United States or became a member of the country.

My mom says all Americans have the right to vote.

Everyone can vote, no matter who they are or

where they live.

A long time ago, some people didn't have this right.

African Americans and women couldn't vote

for a long time. This wasn't fair.

Our leaders changed the law so everybody could vote. Now, everybody is **equal**. This is the best part of being an American.

My mom votes whenever we have an election. It shows that she loves her country. I can't wait until I can vote!

Glossary

booth (BOOTH) A small closed space.

candidate (KAN-duh-dayt) Somebody who runs in an election.

election (ih-LEHK-shun) The act of picking a leader.

equal (EE-kwuhl) When things are the same for everybody.

speech (SPEECH) A talk to a group of people.

Index

candidate(s), 10, 11, 12, 16

citizen, 18

elect(ing), 6, 8

elected, 8, 10

election(s), 14, 16, 22

Election Day, 13, 15

equal, 21

ideas, 11

leader(s), 6, 7, 8, 9, 10, 21

president, 8

rules and laws, 7

speeches, 11

state, 9

towns and cities, 9

voting, 4, 7, 17

voting booth, 14